I
I'll Testify!

Autobiography
God Preserves and Prepares for His Purpose
Rev. Dr. Mary Elizabeth LeSure, CPE

ISBN-13: 978-1983402456

Front and Back Cover Photographs
taken by my neighbor, Suzanne.

Chapter One

God Preserves His People

Chapter Two

God Prepares His People

Chapter Three

Gods' Purpose for His People

All Glory and Honor Belongs to

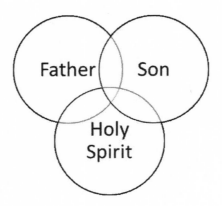

My Heavenly Father, I love You. Thank You, for Your Divine preservation, planned preparation and Your ultimate purpose for my life. Jesus, thank You for the Gifts You freely give me. I pray and strive for souls to be saved, as You have saved me. Holy Spirit because You empower me, lives will be transformed. My hope is to glorify You, by living obediently.

Commemoration of

Bernice J. Bowen

Mama, you taught me faith-walk by praiseworthy. Your words of wisdom came from God, and reached a multitude of hearts. Mama, you knew how to give love to everyone. You practiced how to receive joy and peace from people and God. You are blessed and highly favored.

Dedications

To my handsome husband. We have lived through pain and prosperity. The closer we get to God; the closer we are to each other. You are my close friend, my covering, and soul-mate. Thanks for unfailing encouragement. I love you.

To my darling children; Michael Scott, Frank Jr., Monika Komika and Matthew DeVon and your dear families, you are in my most secret prayers. My heart's desire is that you truly know Jesus and live God's purpose for your life.

To all my beautiful grandchildren; may the blessings of the Lord be upon you, and overtake you in every area of your long lives. Seek the Lord while you are young, and trust Him all the days of your life. Remember Granddad and Grandma loves you and so does Jesus.

To my beloved brothers and sisters; Rosie Lee, Shirley Ann, David Daniel, and Jeffery Earl; we will always remember Mama. She is the tie that binds us. Let us be faithful to God, until that Glorious Appearing of Christ and our eternal life.

To Beverly Ann, we have been down the road, and back again. Thank you for sharing your life with me. You are my BF Forever.

To my esteemed Professors, Executive Director and Dean of Education of Destiny; I will spread seeds of H.O.P.E., wherever I go.

To ministries I have labored with; your kindness and open doors allow my life's purpose to bloom. Thank you for trusting me with your sheep.

And to everyone who read this book; God Bless you with all spiritual blessings in Christ Jesus. It is His will and good pleasure for us to be His children.

Words could not express the things that I have gone through and the things that I'm still learning about faith and its' true meaning.

Growing up as a child faith was not a priority in my home. I never knew what it felt like to wake up on Sunday mornings and prepare myself for church. My junior high school year was the first time I actually was baptized and felt like I belong to a church home.

I do know now. I have two wonderful people in my life that walk and talk by faith. I can always get advice and understanding about what it's like to be a true Christian.

So, I thank Jesus every day for bringing Elder Eddie LeSure Sr., and Evangelist Mary LeSure into my life. For I know, they will guide me in understanding how to walk by faith. In my future, there is a lot that I need to learn in order to become a true Christian. In order to bring Jesus into my life, I have to bring Him into my home.

I also need to be taught how to love Him unconditionally, without questioning my faith. Without Evangelist Mary LeSure, and her family I still would be struggling with understanding of how to begin walking by faith.

Rosalyn Rainey

Chapter One

Caterpillar

God Preserves His People

God's Goodness and Mercy

God Preserves His People

Butterflies develop through a metamorphic change. Metamorphosis is a Greek word for transformation. Adult females lay an egg on a plant. Within five days, caterpillars form while incubated inside the egg.

The caterpillar eats through the egg surface and break out onto the leaf. The plant becomes its food. They are 0.1 inches long and weigh only 1/16 of a pound.

Both caterpillars and babies are tiny in size. My fragile beginning needed God's Divine protection for preservation. Born prematurely, my weight was less than three pounds.

The following testimonies are some of the ways God mercifully intervened and conserved my life for His Glory. He knew, before I was born, that I would tell of His Goodness and Mercy.

Surely,

Goodness and Mercy

shall follow me,

all the days of my life.

Psalm 23a

My spiritual conversion from sinner to Saint, is similar the caterpillar's metamorphose to a butterfly. This chapter shares how God preserved me on my journey.

Think Back on All the Ways God has Preserved
Your Life, Jot Down Your Blessings.

_____

_____

_____

_____

_____

_____

_____

_____

_____

_____

_____

_____

Blessed at Birth

The Word of The Lord came me, saying,

Before I formed thee in the belly,

I knew thee;

Before thou came forth out of the womb,

I sanctified thee,

I ordained thee

Jeremiah 1:4

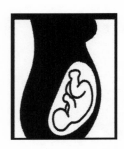 I was born two months premature. My birthday was God's gestation time. Mama said, I was so small she, carried me on a bed pillow. In appreciation to God, she called me her 'miracle baby'.

Preemies' who survived a day or two were labeled 'weaklings'. Infants were placed in machines similar to the farm poultry incubators. Over or under heated incubators caused fatal errors, but

that was the only hope for doomed babies. Oxygen saved lives but unregulated use was detrimental.

> *A new condition, *retrolental fibroplasia, or RLF, disorder of the retinal vasculature, became a leading cause of child blindness in the U.S.*
> Reedy, page 1

I was incubated in intensive care immediately after delivery. I thank God, for protecting me, just as He did the Hebrew boys in the fiery furnace. I was not burned alive! Nor did I suffer long term nerve cell damage; as of some precious preemies.

The flow of oxygen seeped into my eye. The retina did not fully develop and it detached from my pupil. RLF damaged my eyesight. I have no light or vision in my right eye. Those fumes could have permeated both delicate eyes. I might have been totally blind. God preserved my left eye from harmful oxygen gases. I am blessed to have corrected left eye sight to see my way through life.

But God,

but God,

but God!

God knew His purpose for us before creating us. He loves us and has wonderful plans for our life. He is perfect and proactive in planning.

before I or you were formed in our Mother's belly, God preserved us.

Journal How God Preserved

You from Birth or Infancy

_____

_____

_____

_____

_____

_____

_____

_____

_____

_____

_____

_____

Playing with Poison

 My inquisitive toddler stage was filled with discovery. I amused inquisitively with toys. I fondled whatever objects reachable, and encountered all kinds of stuff in the house.

Mama revealed, she would catch me finger-picking at the window sills and plastered walls. I was eating paint. She had to slap my little hands, when she found me repeatedly consuming paint.

Lead is a metal and toxic to humans. Chronic poisoning occurs in children who ingest the metallic lead. I gnawed on lead painted surfaces.

Poisons accumulate by multiple exposures. Impurities can affect developing nervous systems. Digested lead polluted my blood system. Contamination can also lead to brain development or muscle impairment.

Lead   Encephalopathy   follows absorption of a large amount of lead. Initial clumsiness, vertigo, ataxia with a progression of vomiting, and coma . . . there   is   sudden   increased intracranial   pressure.   25%   of poisoned will die. Half the survivors show evidence of permanent damage to the central nervous system, mental retardation and palsy.

Tabher's

Mama told me how my body swole twice its size. Back to intensive care for me! She described how doctors gave me ice baths for high temperatures. They shaved my head and put tubes under the skull skin. Doctors drained excess fluids within my cranium.

As a young adult, I asked my dentist, why I had those wavy, tinged niches in my lower front teeth. He said, I must have had a remarkably high temperature, before my permanent teeth came. My teeth were acutely damaged, by my body heat, prior to growing out of my gums. The Lord wondrously brought me out, again!!

And, if they drink any deadly thing,
it shall not hurt them.
Mark 16:18

There is an adage; God has mercy on fools and babies. I was a baby and did not know the harm I was doing to my body or, eating deadly lead paint.

Give an Account of How God Brought
You Out Safely, as A Toddler

_____

_____

_____

_____

_____

_____

_____

_____

_____

_____

Bounced-off a Buick!

At elementary age, one playful day, coming home from school, I was not watching where I going. I was hit by a car. The jet black, pug nosed, Buick was not going fast or, it would have run over me.

Holding on to the shiny, silver hood-ornament, was my life-line. The driver slammed the brakes, stopping the 4,000 pound car in its tracks.

I was sprung off the hood, tumbling to the tarred gravel road. I scrambled to my knees. I picked up my ultra-thick glasses and wobbled to my feet. I was stunned and dazed with skin scraped limbs.

My primary fright was being in trouble with Mama. She had told me, time and time again, about walking in the street. It was a not-to-do thing. Tommy Lee, a neighbor boy, and I raced to my house, tell her about the bump accident.

Cast down, but not destroyed.
II Corinthians 4:*9*

The Lord held back what could have been an unfortunate tragedy.

But God,
but God,
but God!

preserves us for His use. If we allow Him; He prepares us for His plan. Each person can choose God's purpose for his or her life.

Share an Accident, When God Kept

You During Your Elementary Years

_____

_____

_____

_____

_____

_____

_____

_____

_____

_____

Frightful Freeway Ride

An independent outing to the movie theater was a big deal for me at fifteen. While waiting for the city bus, a car with two men pulled up to the corner and stopped. One male asked, "Where are you going?" I told them of my exciting plan. I was offered a ride.

Thinking I'd get there faster and save money; I unwittingly got in the car. After reaching the turn toward the cinema, they went the other way. I pleaded to get out of the auto, to no avail. They were smoking something that smelt like dry hay.

I heard them talk about a train, but I didn't see any railroad tracks. I was fearfully begging and crying to go home. A guy said, "Lie down on the back seat and be quiet!" They pulled under a viaduct; the sign read 'Willow Springs'. We road about an hour. One fellow talked the other into taking me back to the bus stop.

By God' Grace, neither man touched my trembling body or raped me. They drove me back to the Hill and released me from the car. One man sternly instructed me to *"never get in a car with strangers"*. From that day to this, I took his strong advice.

I ran, lickety-split all the way home. Knowing; except for the Grace of God, I could have been easily missing, abused and killed!

Tell How God Protected You
from Danger in Your Teenage Years

_____

_____

_____

_____

_____

_____

_____

_____

_____

_____

_____

Born-again, Free at Last

My husband, Eddie and I joined a church 1972. The atmosphere was traditional formalities and social activities. The sermons had smidgens of salvation. There was no conviction of sin or instruction for holy living. We sat in the parking lot, smoking marijuana joints, before entering the sanctuary.

We were good participants. I was in the adult choir. Eddie was on the Deacon board. We were faithful church members for twelve years. We were good people; taking care of home, family and career jobs. Demonstrating morally good works, but not saved.

The god of this world hath blinded the minds of
them which believe not, in case
The Light of the glorious gospel of Christ,
Who is the image of God, should shine unto them.
I Corinthians 4:4

Satan has been on the rampage to deceive mankind since the Garden of Eden. But, El-Elyon, The Most High God, has given us faith. Faith is trust 'in' God. Faith gives spiritual sight to the heart of unbelief.

My addiction to drugs began on my 23rd 'golden' birthday, during a gift-trip to St. Louis. While riding, LeSure offered me a joint, for the umpteenth time. I told him *No*, again. I didn't even take aspirin.

I rebutted, snubbing: *"Something that small won't effect on me!"* He called my bluff. We went back and forth. I ignored, stating I didn't even like the smell. I referred to the times he would smoke at home I insisted he go in our basement.

Finally, after hearing I was afraid, I took the dare. I took the lit refer and puffed. I was instructed to hold the smoke in as long as I could. I held the smolder in my lungs and had a sense of well-being.

The sensation of euphoria caused me to recline in my seat. I relaxed. I heard my clear voice plunge several pitches. The drizzling rain on the windshield was exaggerated to a deluge. And, I had an overwhelming desire to stop the car and have sex. So, we did.

Seven years later, I smoked Kool-long cigarettes daily. When I was too lazy to go to the store and get a carton, I would reach under the bed and twists a couple used butts together and make-do.

I snorted cocaine for recreation on a regular basis. And, popped speed just to *do* more and they gave me lots of energy to go at a faster pace. I indulged in black-beauties which curbed my appetite and put me in a real good mood. Hashish a drug made from cannabis and many other illicit drugs were in my goody bag.

There was no law against smoking at work, so I smoked at my desk. I chain-smoked, to the tune of three packs per day. Many of the cigarettes burnt up in the ashtray, but I smoked my share. I tried to quit smoking cigarettes several times. They were going up in price, from thirty-five cents to fifty cents per pack. I didn't want to pay that!

I and some of the girls Wilma, Joyce, Debra ~ would get *high* in the ladies restroom. Our group, of working clericals, had a steady diet of alcoholic beverages, during happy hour at the neighborhood bar. It was a regular meeting place after work. Sometimes I supplied drugs for my friends. I didn't have to pay money for any narcotics because my hubby *was* the 'drug dealer'. He had suitcases full. The real cost was the price of my soul. I thought, "*there must be more, to life*", than vices that bound me. In my late twenties, my sister, Rosie, boldly told me:

> *"Mae,*
>
> *if you don't get saved,*
>
> *you're going to Hell!"*

I bogusly prayed with her to stop the nagging. I foolishly went my sinful way. I wasn't the first to reject Jesus, His messenger or His message.

Jesus took rejection from the wayward world, which loved darkness. Jesus was refused by the people of Israel. Jesus was disowned by His family and the scorned by religious community.

The Lord was abandoned by those who received His healing and deliverance. Jesus took His disciples as confidants and showed them special miracles. Christ was even deserted by them who walked with Him and seen His ministry in action. The unchurched individual is often more susceptible to receiving the Truth of God, than a staunch churchgoer.

January 16, 1983, my husband and three children were at church. My one week old son, Matthew, was in his bassinette. His name means Gift of God. I had my tubes tied the day after he was born. In my selfishness I did not want any more children. I wanted to continue to fly across the country with LeSure and his magic suitcase.

While taking a sitz bath and smoking marijuana, I wrestled within. No matter how many joints I smoked I couldn't get high. My sister's haunting words rang in my ears and in my spirit. I couldn't enjoy getting high. I was disturbed.

"Mae,
if you don't get saved,
you're going to
Hell!"

I sensed Hell's fire under my claw-foot tub! Hastily, I hurdled out my tub, sprinted to my bedside, and collapsed to my knees. I said,

"Jesus,
'If' You are *really real*,
Come into my heart."

HE DID IT. . .
JESUS SAVED ME!!

Right then and there, Jesus heard my prayer, forgave my sins, and saved my soul! He miraculously washed me in His Blood. He is a Mighty Deliverer and Wonderful Savior. I literally felt burdens lift from my shoulder blades. Strongholds that had me bound; were broken! I was Saved and Delivered!!

> *Satanic influences can range from temptation to total domination. Temptation can be resisted by a simple prayer. Deliverance is used when people earnestly desire to be freed from apparent demonic influence in some area of their lives.*
> Collins

Immediately, I prayed that my husband and children would accept Jesus. I wanted everyone to have the *freedom* I was experiencing. Intercession was my new normal. Holy Spirit gave me passion for others.

I leaped to my feet, ran to my dresser. I took my pound of 'gold-bud' stash, and quickly flushed it down the toilet. I was *Free*; devoid of the process of gradually weaning from drugs. I did not have the physical and emotional problems experienced with withdrawal of a person dependent on a substance. Jesus delivered me and my husband that week! LeSure says,

> "He reached down on the inside
> and took away the taste of drugs."

I need the assistance in recovering by rehabilitation. We didn't *quit* using drugs; we were immediately delivered by the power of God through prayer. Yes, Jesus took away the desire for the taste of my addictions. Christ called me out from a life of unbelief and blatant sin, of pleasing this flesh. Jesus changed my mind, heart and life.

Being a sinner is not just what we do
more importantly,
it is our spiritual position at birth.

But, even if I had never smoked, drank or committed a wrong act; I, you and all mankind need to be saved. After The Fall in the Garden of Eden, humans were born sinners because Adam chose to obey Satan. That choice corrupted all humans through the bloodline.

Share How Your Life Has Changed by
Someone that Witnessed to you About God.

_____

_____

_____

_____

_____

_____

_____

_____

_____

_____

_____

Receiving Christ Easy as ABC

Admit that you have sinned.

Believe that Jesus died to free you from your sins.

Confess your sin to God and accept Jesus as Savior.

<u>You can pray this prayer</u>
<u>and accept Jesus as Savior</u>

Dear God,

I know that I am a sinner.

I believe that Jesus died for my sins.

I believe Jesus rose from the grave.

I now turn from all my sins.

Jesus please forgive me for my sins.

Jesus, I invite You into my heart.

Jesus please change my life.

Jesus I receive You as my personal Savior.

Jesus help me follow You as Lord.

Thank You Jesus, for forgiving me,

Thank You Jesus, for saving me.

In Jesus name I pray.

Amen.

If you sincerely believe, what you prayed, you are
saved. By Faith we receive the Promises of God.
Now, run and tell that!

Testify of When, Where and How
Jesus Christ Saved Your Soul

Filled with The Holy Ghost

Satan's assigned demons constantly pestered me. I dreamed about smoking and awoke with the taste of nicotine in my mouth.

The sensations were so real, I could smell and taste tobacco. I physically sat on my hands, in my dining room chair, praying to not smoke.

> *Demonic forces are resisted in the name of Jesus Christ and commanded to leave.*

> *The change is likely to be temporary unless there is a filling with the Holy Spirit and commitment to practicing spiritual disciplines.* Collins:

I knew I did not have the power to free myself, but God did. I trust Him. The Word gives instructions on how to resist temptation in James 4:7

Submit yourselves to God,
resist the devil and
he will run away from you.

 Persistently, I kneeled at the church altar. I cried and asked Jesus to fill me with the Holy Ghost. I had grid marks imprinted on my knees, from floor intake vents. On March 9, 1983, a traveling Evangelist taught how to receive Holy Spirit.

He illustrated by throwing a set of keys, and instructed someone to catch them, then threw them again and allowed them land on the floor. The Evangelist said,

"Receiving the Holy Ghost is just like that;
He is here, waiting to be received."

The crusader invited people to the altar for prayer. He laid hands on people praying to receive Holy Spirit. I was in line. I *expected* to receive.

I was praising God, prior to the minister making his round to me. When he touched my throat, my words of adoration to God, turned into unknown words. Hallelujah! I *saw* the letters changing as they came up out of my spirit. I spoke in awe and thanksgiving but,

I was speaking in another tongue!
Holy Spirit was dwelling inside me!

My very soul was rejoicing and my heart was glad. The wide mouth grin on my face could not be erased. I had keeping power to live my Christian life. God completely freed me from that nicotine addiction. The things I used to do; I didn't want to do any more. The evil desire was gone. Holy Spirit began teaching me righteous upright living.

I have my own SWAT
(Special Weapons and Tactics)
S a v e d **W** i t h **A** **T** e s t i m o n y

Be a Witness of Your Experience

in Receiving Holy Spirit.

_____

_____

_____

_____

_____

_____

_____

_____

_____

_____

_____

_____

_____

Distressful Disc

My leg was hurting up and down,
Even when I happy, I wore a frown.
It was hard to sit, walk, or stand,
To get any relief, I went to sleepy-pie land.

I came to your office that faithful day,
Hoping you would take my pain away.
You gave me an electromyogram test,
It felt like electrocution - at best.

You requested magnetic resonance imaging,
EMG & my description, then you named the thing.
The diagnosis was L5-S1 herniated disc,
Surgery was recommended - there was little risk.

With that news, my eyes swelled with a few tears,
the urgency of the matter left no room for fears.
I took your prescribed pain pills and advice too,
because I believed you knew what I should do.
I am blessed to say all is fine,

Thanks Dr. Wolf,

God used you to help me,

That's the way He is because,

God is Good . . .

. . . All the time!

Sonnet for Wolf, D.O.

September, 1998

When Has God Guided You
to The Right Place For Help?

_____

_____

_____

_____

_____

_____

_____

_____

_____

_____

_____

Surprise Surgery, Surprised!

Dr. Wolf referred me to your care,
I wondered what you'd say when I got there.
You reviewed the MRI of my lumbar spine,
then got right to the point with no waste of time.

It was indicated via your backbone double,
the disc-herniation, L5-S1 was serious trouble.
Within seven days; your question was to me,
"Whether or not I would have surgery?"

I elected to go under the knife,
literally putting in your hands, my life.
I prayed for me and for you too ~
that God would show you what to do.

Your skill and knowledge was a true success
the Lord Jesus was with us and that's not a guess.
I follow your instructions to stay on track
because, I don't want any set back.

I was gratefully surprised when I got my bill,

you discounted the surgical amount ~ what a thrill!

Thank you Dr. Brayton, you've been so very kind;

Thank God too 'cause

God is Good . . .

. . . All the time!

Ode to Brayton, M.D.

September 1998

When Did You Trust God Enough to
Put Your Life in Someone's Hands?

_____

_____

_____

_____

_____

_____

_____

_____

_____

_____

_____

Mary's Medical Miracle

On Memorial Day weekend 2006, I flew to visit family in Philadelphia. I went straight to Shirley's house. My sister is a hostess extraordinaire. She receives and entertains guests with a yawl come-back attitude.

Our son Michael, was the grill chief. The cook-out meal was delicious; but I had trouble swallowing. I ate smaller bites and chewed longer, but food painfully scratched my throat. Softer grubs sorely passed my esophagus. Drinks did not help flush the meal or relieve injurious scratches.

There was relentless burning in my genital area. I thought I had a unitary track infection. I didn't have an antibiotic prescription so, I brought some vaginal cream to dismiss the charring. It was a temporary help. Many hot showers, in Shirley's spa-like bathroom briefly comforted the sear.

After bargain hunts, pedicures and manicures we were bushed. I choose to sleep downstairs at Rosie's house or I would have had a beautiful guest room upstairs. My hope was the numerous visits to her powder room would go undetected. I trekked through the night, from the couch, to the bathroom, to the water-cooler repeatedly; no sleep for me.

The next morning, Michael took me shopping in New York City, for millinery supplies. I like going there for bulk inventory. Selections are actually right off the boat. My business name, LeChapeau, follows the origin of my married name. In French, *Le* means *The* and *Chapeau* means *Hat*, tag name: *Gladd Hatter*.

I questioned God, "How can I advertise one-of-a-kind hats?" Holy Spirit told me God *is* the Creator. He created the stars, snowflakes and people all one-of-a-kind, He would help me. He did just that. I produced hats galore.

DeSigns brimmed with confidence. They comprised of no-brim to titanic styles. Wide-brim hats displayed whirls of horsehair and hanging beads. Mid-sized beauties showcased various illuminant pearls and swirls. Perky top cloches sported feathers and life-like flowers. Free-form flairs had brilliant colors with fascinating trims. The *LeChapeau* collection included church, casual and western hats. It was an exciting venture. I did have my hay-days. My advertising motto is:

"If you have a head . . .
. . . *LeChapeau* has a hat for you!"

I catered house visits, hosts invited guests to private showings to buy hats in the comfort of their home. I exhibited at religious and secular conventions. My fashion shows traveled interstate.

My entrepreneur business included proprietor of two hat boutiques, in different cities. That was a dream come true. The Beacon News took pictures and printed a full page ad of my unique boutique. I had opportunities to guide novice hat-makers. I mentored etiquette by consulting protégés how to behave in various social situations. My Scripture is:

Whatsoever thy hand finds to do,
do it with all thy might.
Ecclesiastes 9:10

After shopping I spent the night at Mikes' bachelor pad. He is a career military man with three tours of duty overseas. Michael has honorably served in Panama, Kuwait and Afghanistan for our country. His decor senses are minimalistic, no knick-knacks just sandy, chocolate and green; very clean and neat. If only I could have rested. Quietly, I rounded his bedroom to the living room corner, went through the kitchen, to the bathroom; several times that night.

The next morning, Michael took me shopping in New York City for millinery supplies. I felt hungry but ate little; mostly drinks and potty brakes. I was weak, unbalanced and almost dragging. I relied on his strong arm for walking support. One last rest stop on the Turnpike, then back to PA.

The following day, Michael and his fiancée Felicia, dropped me at the Philadelphia International Airport. I was headed to my connection flight in Detroit. It was a beautiful airport. There were many mall-type stores, lots of specialty shops and a gazillion fast food places. I shopped kiosks and loaded up on things to relieve my symptoms. I brought sweet drinks and orange sherbet. I visited every bathroom in route to the boarding gate and lined up with *those who needed assistance.*

I kindly asked the man in the middle to change seats with me, explaining my need for excessive bathroom breaks. I offered him my window seat. He said "sure, not a problem." The man in the aisle seat did not move, but he was co-operative to let me in and out for restroom runs.

The Detroit Metropolitan Airport is so big, it has a train that runs through the main terminal of the depot. It is the second largest terminal in the world. I rode a metro shuttle rail-train, called *Express Tram*. Down below, I saw groups of people sitting at boarding gates waiting on their flight.

The voice on the intercom announced the gate where I should exit the train. I got off. I watched the candy-apple red train  move on the strip. It looked like a toy; too small for anyone to fit inside. Dazed and supportably leaning on my luggage, I watched it was out of sight. My perception was not reality. Something was exceptionally wrong with me. Slowly entering a walking conveyor I experienced stumbling dizziness. I held the banister to keep from falling. My self-control was about to collapse. I felt jittery. My body ached all over and muscles were growing limp. I saw a Red Cap attendant with a wheelchair. I was happy to see help! I asked him to assist me and give me a ride to my gate. He was cordial, but not helpful. He informed me that service had to be 'called for' in advance.

Disappointed, weak and somewhat confused, I sat a while, walked bit, rested a little, used the bathroom a lot; repeat. I was running out of time to make my connection to Chicago. My vision was blurred and my nervous system had uncontrollable shakes. What was wrong with me? I prayed;

"Lord, I need your strength."

Boarding the plane to Chicago, as in Philadelphia, I loaded with the 'assistance needed' passengers and traded my window seat for the aisle seat. The persistent walks to the washroom were feebly made. I prayed in my mind . . . then thought, I better pray with my voice so, I prayed out loud;

"Lord, I Need Your Strength!"

The Word of God gives me confidence
He will order His angels
to protect you wherever you go.
Psalm 91:11

LeSure picked me up at Chicago Midway Airport, domestic baggage claim. I saw him descending on the escalator. He appeared to be gliding on air. I couldn't understand how he reached me without walking. Delusively, he was floating. He gently aided me to the car, and asked "What's wrong Baby?" I wasn't sure, but, didn't feel good. I slept most of the hour drive to Aurora. LeSure stopped at a store. I used the restroom, brought snacks and sit outside on a bench. The neon lights were harshly bright. My weakness caused him to almost carry me to the car.

Finally, home. I sat on the side of our elevated bed. The 7up and sherbet were cooling to my inners. It felt like I was having an organ meltdown. The last thing I remember is a big drool on my blouse.

The next day, Eddie, he had tried to rouse me, by calling my name, and shaking me but, he didn't get a response. Years later, in a worship service he testified of that morning saying:

"Her eyes were rolled back
with only white showing,
her arms were crossed on her chest,
her lips were purple and she wasn't breathing."

He was terrified and prayed for God to help him, help me. He didn't get any cooperation when bathing or fully dressing me. I became aware of my change of clothes by a misstep on the curb, going inside the clinic.

I don't recall climbing in the emergency truck. I was jarred when I heard loud banging on the ambulance door. LeSure yelled, "What are you doing in there?" His tone was frantic. His urgency bolted me to consciousness. My body received hydration. Speeding to the hospital, paramedics worked to find a viable flowing blood vessel. The small veins kept collapsing and *moving*.

There are tiny blood vessels just under the skin and larger veins to draw blood. When the needle is inserted vessels may be injured and bleeding occurs. Bruising is caused when injury to blood vessels leak blood. Shortly, the surface skin of my hands and arms were crimson-purple from probing.

The hallucinations kept coming. I could see out the top of my head! A smooth face invited me to a place of serenity. He or she was hairless, no brows or lashes. A welcoming countenance smiled, amidst a circumference of rainbow rays. It was absolutely beautiful. I felt no pain.

Oxygen was administered in the hospital emergency room. Technicians placed heart monitors to my chest and attached an insulin drip. Dr. Khan and team, worked relentlessly to resolve my grave condition. I was in critical care three days and hospitalized for seven days. A slew of tests were performed on my near lifeless body, diseased blood and cloudy urine. My blood-glucose was near the Guinness Book of World Records:

My A1C was 16 and
my blood glucose level was
a death defying 2,165!

I began to come to my senses in ICU. I saw a lime green stool grow in elevation in the corner of my room. I franticly called the attendant. He said, my electrolyte imbalance caused graphic hallucinations then added,

"People on the street pay good money to see what you saw."

My diagnosis was hyperosmolar hyperglycemia; an abnormal high concentration of sugar in the blood, onset diabetes mellitus type 2, commonly known as *sugar diabetes*. I was not aware of a pre-disposition to the disease, being border-line, or of its' chronic nature. I thought I would get cured in the hospital, go home and forget all about this, diabetes thing.

Doctor analysis included pneumonia, bacterium inflammation of my lungs right base. Also reported was anxiety, the condition of living under distress. Psychological tension deprives the body of strength, influence thoughts, and produces sickness.

An intensive-care technician sang a medley of phases in my hospital room.

'Swing Low Sweet Chariot' and *'Sugar, Sugar, You Are My Candy Girl'*

Apparently, that was his manner of passing time. I let him know the chariot was *not* coming to take me away that day! Holy Spirit told me:

> *I will not die but live,*
> *and will proclaim*
> *what the LORD has done!*
> Psalm 118:17

Doctors, nurses, technicians and aides came to my bedside; shaking their heads in disbelief of my survival. Saying, "So, you're *the one* with that high glucose reading!" Some attendees verged applauding. Truly, I thank God for the health care professionals who worked to salvage me. And, for waking my loving husband to pray, bathe, dress, and get medical attention for me.

The Lord guided LeSure.
He listened to and obeyed Holy Spirit
in the crucial steps to help save my life.

Eddie's love and care had been with me at other times of sickness and surgery. He has a very pleasant bedside manner. But in this life and death time of distress, he showed himself to be unconditionally faithful.

I was blessed with many well-wishers and visitors. When my David and Sandra came to visit me at the hospital, they looked like angels. My best friend Beverly and my dear Mom cooked and froze food for our household. Even while lying in the bed the aromas filled my senses. Later, Eddie served me on china dishes.

My church home, Covenant of Faith, nourished me back to health by suppling catered meals. I was so grateful, I gave them a plaque. Brother and Sister Wiggins are Jamaican chefs with a catering business. They brought me of their specialties on a weekly basis. What a delicious blessing!

I share my medical miracle to declare God's power over sickness. He has preserved me for His purpose. By His Grace, I am alive to witness His amazing Power. God, Jehovah-Rapha, healed my body, soul and spirit, and then allowed me to ~ "Run On!"

Glorify God, by Telling How

He Alone Has Power to Sustain Your Life.

_____

_____

_____

_____

_____

_____

_____

_____

_____

_____

_____

_____

Psalm of Favor

Your favor opens invisible doors and
grants my rest on peaceful shores.
Your favor to me is sweet I know
You fill my life with Your glow.

Your favor gives me strength to stand,
when I'm reeling in a barren land.
Your favor to me is sweet I know
You fill my life with Your glow.

Sweet Jesus, Your blood has paid the price,
I will live to Your glory, and get to paradise.
Your favor to me is sweet I know
You fill my life with Your glow.

Your favor is not for me alone,
but to all I meet it must be shown.
Your favor to me is sweet I know
You fill my life with Your glow.

You are my wonderful Savior, mighty Deliver,

my perfect Counselor and complete Healer.

Your favor to me is sweet I know

You fill my life with Your glow.

Your truth penetrates my very soul,

Your delicious favor girds me to be bold.

Your favor to me is sweet I know

You fill my life with Your glow.

Write a Love Letter to God, for Who He is, for Things He Has Done, and Is Doing, for You.

_____

_____

_____

_____

_____

_____

_____

_____

_____

_____

_____

_____

Chapter Two

Larva

God Prepares His People

Learning God's Ways

God Prepares His People

In the larva stage caterpillars stop eating, spins a silky cocoon, and lives in it. The cocoon protects the young invertebrate. The larva has no backbone and is immobile during this juncture. Radical transformation takes place during this crucial period. The insect undergo changes to its slim body and develops wings. When conversion is over; the worm will emerge an adult butterfly!

I straddled two lifestyles; staunch church-goer and wanton sinner. I was loyal to singing in the choir but, my sinful behavior was immoral.

My metamorphosis started with an urgent warning from a saint. Later, I trusted Jesus as Savior. Then, I received the gift of Holy Spirit. I began a progressive transformation.

Like a cocoon, Holy Spirit, wrapped my soul in His powerful protection. Larvae have a non-

feeding stage.   Differing, I begin devouring the
Word of God, learning righteousness, judgment
and true holiness.

Journal Ways God Has Prepared You
to Serve His People

_____

_____

_____

_____

_____

_____

_____

_____

_____

_____

_____

_____

The Good Ole Days!

My family progenitors are from Covington, Tennessee. My parents met as teenagers, respectfully courted and soon married. They migrated to Illinois and settled in Will County. Riley's Hill is a small unincorporated area between Joliet and Lockport. The village bypass, Collins Street, made a path through property of Illinois State Penitentiary.

Daddy would take us down *The Hill*, joy riding. It was aptly named due to a nearly 45 degree incline. After turning the corner on Arthur Avenue, he mashed the gas pedal and *Zoooom*! My stomach dropped to my toes. We were boosted a couple inches from the car seat. Us kids, were  filled with excited fear ~ better known as a thrill. Yeah! Three sets of railroad tracks were constructed at the end of the slope and gave an additional rise. Daddy sped over the course;

bumpily, bumpily, bump. Childish glees filled the car. Wee! Wee!!

My Dad had the most beautiful penmanship. He wrote in the *Old English* style. I saw (and secretly read) some of the manuscripts he wrote to Mama. They were adult words of love. I wish I had kept some of his writings. I endeavored to mimic his handwriting. My fifth grade teacher, Mrs. McDaniel, told me, "When you get out of school, you can write the way you want. But, for then I had to cursive write the way she was teaching. It's a shame that many schools have taken cursive writing out of curriculum.

Daddy creatively provided a home for us in a repurposed railroad boxcar. Story goes, he won it in a card game and had some friends tow it up to The Hill. Inside was a kid's bedroom, and dining room/kitchen combo. Our freight-car home had three rooms annexed on front. Daddy built them. They were covered with tar paper. Children in a home of love do not know they are poor. There was no feeling of depravity due to lack of running water or central heat.

We used a potbellied coal stove to cook and stay warm. We pumped well water, raised baby chicks, grew garden vegetables, used a wooden outhouse, romped in the prison field, and made mud pies. It was a good life. I call them good old days!

Mama survived the hardship and painful deaths of three husbands. She gave birth to eight children, five bouncing boys and three giggly girls. She worked at home and was there for family. We were disciplined with long informative lectures and or a whopping.

Once, Mama *thought* I did something wrong that warranted a lashing. I got it! Case and point ~ I had a Mothers' Day gift on lay-a-way. It is a gold ring with her, and my siblings birthstone gems inset. After work I went to pay on the account. I was late getting home. It was pass sunset. I had to get my own switch from the pussy-willow tree, across the street in Mr. Hido's yard, (that's where we got our well water). Then, bring the tool of my punishment back to the house, put it in her hand, and suffer the accused consequences. I didn't spoil her surprise by telling why I got home late. But, I yet remember that beating.

The long willow switch was drawn back over Mama's shoulder. It whistled through the air with lighting speed and wrapped around my legs. I you, it's not a good thing to run into the closet when getting whooped. That corner was not a refuge for me. Ouch!

She trained her children well. We all love her dearly. Now grown, my siblings and I work to keep close family ties regardless of living in different states. We are united by communal empathy. When one hurts each of us feel the pain. Our training included the importance of going church and being a committed member. Mama instructed us go get a good education. Each of us strive to attain personal best. We actively encourage each other's prosperity and good health.

Think About Some of Your Good Ole Days
Growing Up, Smile and Write Them Down.

_____

_____

_____

_____

_____

_____

_____

_____

_____

_____

_____

Wash, Rinse, and Dry

We were taught how to keep house. We did laundry in an automatic ringer-washer. The water was run into the basin tub and Tide detergent, Clorox bleach and Arm and Hammer baking-soda was included. The cleaning agents were allowed to agitate before the dirty clothes were submerged. It was a time consuming process, but we had spotless clothes.

After soaking several hours or overnight, the clothes were washed. The agitator slowly moves back and forth scrubbing off particles of dirt, food and odors from garments. Without fading or damaging, the clothes are cleaned of dirty scum they held.

Use of the ringer-washer involves running the clothes through a double cylinder. The two rolls squeeze murky water from garbs. Then, we fill up the washer tub with clean water for the rinse.

Once, while feeding laundry through the rollers, my fingers got caught. Shear force pulled my fingers, wrist and forearm up to the elbow, through the pressing mechanism. Dag-nab-it! The joint  between my upper and lower arm popped the rollers open. In fright, I happily pried my arm out. From that point on, my fingers were at a safe distance. In essence rinsing is the final part of washing. It removes soap and impurities. Hydrotherapy agents are added to rinse water to soften and add a scented smell. Even today I love the fragrance of doing laundry.

After washing and rinsing, the final step is drying. We strung our laundry outside on a clothesline. The plastic coated string, (sometime used for double-dutch) was tied between two poles in the backyard. Laundry was hung with wooden clothespins. A wooden plank prop was used to raise the heavy weight up. The items faced the beaming sun. They swayed on the line. Whipped by the breeze, each fiber was permeated with fresh air. The laundry was emptied of all moisture and dampness. When we brought it into the house, it was beautiful, bone dry and smelt like unpolluted sunshine. Take a deep breath and inhale the freshness of clothes cleaned the old fashioned way.

Just like that clothes line; Jesus was lifted up on Calvary as ransom for our sin. His sinless life was without flaw in character or reputation. Jesus came and lived as the perfect example for us to follow. When we accept Him as Savior and Lord, He gives us the power to live Holy. God commands us to live love Him with our whole heart and to love one another. With spiritual cleansing we can witness for the Lord.

Mama could be found brushing her mouthful of large, white, teeth on the back porch. She took her time. She hummed a song and firmly whisked toothbrush bristles, between her teeth and against her gums. I occasionally heard her talk of birds' beauty. She also animatedly conversed with our dog, Blackie. After communing with nature and creatures outside, she washed-up. She put on her stark-white uniform and snowy polished oxfords. The crisp dress did justice to her professional character.

Tell About Some of the Chores
You Were Responsible for Growing Up.

Bernice's Beauty Salon

For nearly five decades Mama owned and operated *'Bernice's Beauty Salon'*. Everyone on The Hill knew Ms. Bernice. She was a vital part of the community. It was a gathering place for fellowship and get a 'do'. Customers loved her work. They showed devotion by patronizing business. People came from miles around; women, girls and men too! Her dexterous fingers would press, curl, wave, and dye, generations of hair. It was a busy spot. She labored tirelessly from dawn until night yielding glorious professional hairstyles.

She worked willingly with her hands,
Proverb 31:13a

The kitchen doubled as a beauty parlor. There was never a strand of hair in the kitchen or our food. We didn't mix dish rags or with beauty shop towels. Tools were for shop use only!

Customers put their head in Mama's capable hands, laying their neck on the shampoo-bowl groove. She took care of business. She skillfully massaged all the sensitive areas of their head to relieve tension. Some clients went to sleep during a shampoo. The hair was thoroughly washed and rinsed twice. The patron's hair was deep conditioned with a creamy treatment. They sat adorned with a plastic cap for about twenty minutes, and rinsed again. After that, she was towel-dried and placed them under the hair dryer.

 After completely drying the hair it was time for the press and curl. Mama methodologically parted the hair forehead to nape, and ear to ear. The quad sectioning started the 'hot-comb' process. Pressing was done with a metal device, with teeth like a comb and wooden handle. The hot comb was place on open fire. When it smoked, it was ready. Using the rounded edge she applied pressure, gently pulling hair, and straightened it

from the root to tip. She kept a dollop of pressing oil on top of her right hand, (she's left-handed), putting dabs of grease on the hair to prevent brittleness. A soft, raggedy towel on the work-table serviced to wipe the hot comb residue between heating's. Pressed hair was so straight it looked slick.

Curling was the next step. Younger customers had bangs, and a pony-tail or in some cases, a duck-end. A good pressing lasted over two weeks. Mature clientele had all-over curls. Marseille curling irons are metal instruments shaped like pliers. The closed part is a round prong with a lip fitting, and long handle. They gave tight, even, beautifully rounded curls when Mama operated them. She divided the hair in small square portions, and grasped it near the root with the Marseille. She fed the hair around the curlers. Then, rolled the handle between her fingers with her left hand, while controlling the hair with her right hand.

Each roll of the handle took up more hair until all the hair was wrapped around the curler. It amazed me to see that action each time it was executed. The  cooled curls yielded a beauty captured accurately only by a camera's eye. The typical style was combed from the forehead to the nape. Mama strategically pushed the hair forward into bellowing waves and ringlet curls. Client's hair was shiny and full-bodied. Customers did not hesitate to look in the mirror and primp with a broad smile. Many times they gave generous tips.

When other procedures of chemical relaxers, cold wave perms and weaves came on the scene Mama managed the new dos'. She kept up with the latest techniques by going to beauty school. She earned her beauticians license and graduated! Mama attended beauty trade shows and participated in hair style shows. I even won a second place trophy in a hair fashion show. *Bernice's' Beauty*

Salon made its mark. Customers were faithful for generations.

One of my chores was to clean the tools of the trade. I sat on the floor, scrubbing combs and brushes. I used a plastic bucket with hot, soapy water. I cleaned hair out of bristles, by vigorously rubbing two brushes together. The hair was translated by motion, to the top of the brush. Then I pulled the embedded hair out and tossed it. The friction continued, until all traces of grease, and dirt were gone. Combs were faster to clean by simply brushing the comb's teeth, up and down. After rinsing the tools were put in Barbasol disinfectant, to be sterilized, later towel-dried.

Mama endured many days of hard work, inhaling smoke and gulping fumes from chemicals. Her uniform eventually included a protective nose and mouth mask. She had surgery to have polyps removed from her throat. Her ankles would swell as a result of prolonged standing. Impressions were embedded in her fingers where the grip of the curlers had made their mark. Mama decided to retire and sell her home, along with four acquired lots around it. A successful entrepreneur, she gave each child a generous financial love offering, from the sale of her property.

My loving Mother moved out of Illinois and many wished her well. She moved to Philadelphia to a neat apartment, in a building owned by my sister, Shirley. When visiting family I wanted my hair done by the best beautician in the whole world; Mama.

Talk About the Self-Discipline and Duties of Your Parent(s) or Those Who Trained You.

_____

_____

_____

_____

_____

_____

_____

_____

_____

_____

_____

_____

_____

A Virtuous Woman

Often, before we left for school, Mama would put a pot of food on the stove. We ate fresh garden greens, buttermilk cornbread, crispy fried chicken and dried beans with thick pot-liquor. Those victuals are good enough to travel back in time. She knows how to put her *'foot in it!'* House windows were stemmed from cooking. We could smell food before hitting the door. Mama real good pies and delicious peach cobbler. Customers were invited to eat. They took the invitation as a bonus to being a patron and friend. Many times she gave away food.

She stretches out her hand to the poor;
she reaches forth her hands to the needy.
Proverbs 31:20

She kept demandingly busy especially around Easter, Mother's Day, Prom, Christmas and, back to school. Regulars had standing appointments. Other people lined up to get a spot or hope for a cancellation. Her skill made her a valuable woman. Mom took care of her household and trusted God in her life. Her character quickened the lives of all she encountered.

At bedtime I saw Mama in a long flannel nightgown on her knees at her bedside. Her head being bowed and resting on folded hands, praying. I heard voice but, could not make out the words. I believe all her children were in her prayers.

We got ready for church on Saturday. We shined our shoes with Vaseline. We bathed in the foot tub and rolled our bangs. Mama did not *send* us to church. She took us to Mount Olive Missionary Baptist Church. We all piled in the car, sometimes arguing about who would sit by the window. I was in choir and youth group. My favorite was Sunday school. I've always liked learning. The lessons about the Bible drew the essence of my being.

Talk About the Values, Wisdom and Love of Your Parent(s) or Those Who Trained You.

_____

_____

_____

_____

_____

_____

_____

_____

_____

_____

_____

_____

Beloved Mother

You trained me up in the way I should go.
You cooked good food and helped me grow.

You whooped my butt, when I did wrong;
You took me to church ~ where I learned a song.

You held me close saying,
"Everything's gonna be alright."
You showed your love, each day and every night.

May your Mother's Day be Happy
May you have Peace and Pleasure too!
May you think of us with Joy,
Oh, how we love you.

May 10, 1998

Recall How You Have Honored Your
Mother, Father or Guardian(s).

_____

_____

_____

_____

_____

_____

_____

_____

_____

_____

_____

_____

From Blind Date to Life Mate

I traveled fifty miles to sleep-over at Judi's house. I met Judi at the Northern Illinois University, Upward Bound Program, in the summer of 1970. The purposes of the camp is to improve academic performance, introduce students' to a college environment, and build their interest and readiness for a university. The program includes a six week residential session.

During my residence at Upward Bound, there were some girls in our dormitory having a lesbian party. Judi and I did not want to do anything to do with that. We did not go. The next morning in their retaliation, we found a bloody Kotex on our door.

I met Excel, a student from Rockford. He and I awkwardly experimented with teenage sex. I became pregnant. That pregnancy broke my mother's heart. It was the first time I remember seeing her cry. I was so very sorry.

I was unmarried and pregnant. Society deemed that condition a sin and a shame. I was out casted from going school. Lockport Central High directed that I finish my senior year at home. I was a devastated.

I was sat down from the choir at church. No longer could I represent the youth of our congregation, in my condition. My new function was to sit on the pew next to my mom.

I was shut away from social functions. I spent my days making clothes for my growing body, on my sewing machine. I learned to sew as a preteen. Hooks Church, in my neighborhood, held a sewing class. Mrs. McFarland was the patient instructor. She said "If you can sew a straight line, you can make anything". I believed her ~ so I did. Her motto was;

"Can't is a lie . . .

. . . you Can if you try!"

As a seamstress, I designed and constructed wedding gowns, prom dresses, usher ensembles, nurse uniforms, ministerial robes, children clothing, and men's suits. I gathered a modeling crew and produced local and interstate high fashion shows. Janelle, Beverly, Corrine, Arlene, and Jeanine were catwalk divas. The shows had an annual trailing. People attending the events bought ensembles that were modeled. All the clothing fit me.

The nights were filled with listening to music on WVON Radio. I memorized every happy or sorrowful word. My chastisement was sober. Godly laws and social morals, along with Mama frowned on my behavior. God tries to protect us from suffering the consequences, of doing things contrary to His will, by instructing to flee fornication.

Today's society allows normalization of immorality of all types and degrees. Many of the behaviors listed in that passage are openly accepted in our land. There is seemingly nothing is wrong with anything. This attitude put people's feelings above the call to holiness. Now, there is no shame in premarital sex or pregnancy. But, according to God's Word the sin is still sin.

The day my baby was born, I walked to the park. It was a cleared field with a few playground pieces. I swung and swayed in the spring wind. Little did I know, I would be giving birth that night. I had a very hard eighteen hour labor.

I could hear the bones of my pelvis stretching. It sounded like the noise of the ice I was chewing, to get moisture in my mouth. What was worse, I felt the excruciating of separating of my joints. Painful child labor is assigned by God as a result of Eve's disobedience in Eden:

To the woman He said,
'I will greatly multiply your pain in childbirth,
in pain you shall bring forth children.
Genesis 3:16

My son, Michael was born on April 26, 1971. His name means gift from God. Although I did not know God as my Father, I was raised in church and wanted to have something to do with Him. Michael's umbilical cord was wrapped around his neck. But, God did not allow Michael to suffer a restricted blood flow, decreased oxygen, a drop in fetal development or death. Thank You Jesus. My mom was with me all the way.

Five months later, on Saturday, September 18, 1971, Judi and I went to a sock hop at Elgin High School. She and her boyfriend Arthur, set me up on blind date. In the dimly lit gymnasium, I was directed toward two male figures. I wasn't sure which was to be my date. So, as with most visual choices; I gravitated to the most appealing.

He stood, six feet-two inches, 140 pounds, wearing an earth brown, brute-knit suit. It fit like a glove. White leather trim streaked its way down his puffed chest, over flat abs, past the slender waist, and squared off at the hips. His elongated legs were covered with mirror spit-shined, black leather, laced boots. The shadowy profile rendered his  body athletically muscular. The eye-catching ensemble was topped off with a chocolate, wide brim fedora and ivory hatband. He was well dressed from head to toe.

His curvy lips opened, flashing a smile; revealing a border of gold on his teeth! People did not have gold trimmed teeth where I came from. Oh, even his captivating name is *LeSure*.

That very night, he said "I'm gonna' marry you!" I thought no matter what this man said I would not be sucked into having another baby without being a wife. Flippantly, I threw my head back and laughed. The guilt of unwed motherhood would not allow me to even hear his advances.

The night went on and we talked and listened to each other. We shared our lives. I told LeSure I had a baby. He told me he had three daughters, Casandra, Kimberly and Sharon. I told him I was blind in one eye. He told me he had upper dentures. Our secrets were in the open.

LeSure pursued. He called me often. We went to movies, out to dinner, the skating rink or on shopping flings. LeSure 'kept company' with me in our living room! Courting was a formal event.

One evening, He came to visit and I was not home. Jeffery, my baby brother, told Mama, "I know where Mae is." Jeff took it upon himself to escort LeSure to a pool-hall/restaurant where I was attending a party. I was surprised to see him. He lived 25 miles away.

Soon after, LeSure guided me to Navarro's Jewelry and brought a gold and diamond ring.   On Saturday, December 18, 1971 (exactly three months after meeting) we wed in my childhood home.   We are still married, over 46+ years and, so are Judi and Arthur.

We were ready for each other.   Compensate for my indiscretion was marriage.   Therefore, when LeSure married me; he became my 'Knight in Shining Armor'.   These influences are clearly present when I discuss relationships with people who have children or grandchildren and are not married.

Whoso finds a wife finds a good thing,
and obtains favor of The Lord.
Proverbs 18:22

LeSure is faithful to our family and friends.   His demeanor is a peacemaking caliber not a brawler;

aka, lover not a fighter. He is kind to acquaintances and a natural putting people at ease. LeSure lives with integrity and stands firm in his convictions to God.

What Were the Circumstances of How You Met
Your Spouse or Significant Other.

_____

_____

_____

_____

_____

_____

_____

_____

_____

_____

Living has taken us through excellent experiences and tumultuous times. Through it all, hell and high water, we truly love each other. We take the good, the bad, and the ugly as part of our lot in life.

> *for better or for worse . . .*
> *in sickness and in health,*
> *to love and to cherish*

I use words from the Traditional Wedding Vows, to share time I spent caring for my husband during his major surgery. His operation consisted of the implant of three titanium discs, a cage and screws in his vertebra. Eddie was hospitalized for a week and has been in rehabilitation for over six weeks. We were so blessed to be visited by dear friends.

In this section hubby will be identified as EL. This documentation is part of my Clinical Pastoral Education personal evaluation report.

These encounters are depicted in real time. We are 600 miles from home and together day and night. We have been gripped by this situation since April 29th, it is now June 19th.

*Guiding – the ability to help a person come to a life decision on their own.

EL faced the decision to try to check himself out of the rehabilitation center prematurely. I helped him to see that there was a high possibility of a setback in healing. He could cause more physical problems. I felt sad that he thought of himself as old and helpless. I helped him be confident in his abilities to get stronger and keep hope alive.

*Reconciling – the ability to help others re-establish relationships.

 At times, we had to re-establish our relationship to a *real* a love posture. We argued about stupid stuff; like why did I move his water to that end of the table. Once, after I was

talking to the doctors, he accused me of *'trying to run the show'*. We had a foolish, bitter argument that went back twenty-five years. I felt furious and wanted to leave EL lying helpless in the hospital bed. But, I pulled myself together, humbly swallowed my pride and lovingly reconciled; for his sake and my benefit.

*Healing – the ability to bind up another's wounds.

I am attentively binding up his wounds. I patiently sit with EL; continually assuring him, of his daily renewed strength. I sing songs to him and to myself. I need the assurance and comfort as much as he does. During his roughest days and nights I speak The Word of God over him. He was in throws of thrashing in the bed. He was talking out of his head and wrenching the covers off his body. He heard my voice through his turmoil. In his sleep, EL repeated Scriptures I recited to him. It felt insecure to see *My Man* in that condition. Yet, I have peace of God that everything will be alright.

*Supporting – thee ability to stand firm with another by holding them in high esteem.

These days it is very important for me to gird EL in high esteem. I let him know he is truly loved, greatly respected and highly valued in my sight. I have given him an Amope pedicure and rubbed him down with lotion. It is my intention to show him the special attention that lets him know he is cared for mentally, physically emotionally and spiritually. His well-being *is* my responsibility.

*Sustaining – the ability to encourage another while they are in the midst of difficult times.

My practice of helping EL sustain a strong psyche has been prevalent for decades. This current difficult situation magnifies that repetition.

Last November, my hubby turned seventy years old. Now that EL is a septuagenarian, his essence is more delicate than ever. He is not a pessimist. His despair is circumstance related. It is miserable and stressful time for him and me.

EL's bedridden state caused him to shrink in the hope of a purposeful future. He called himself worn-out and useless. I assured him that this too, will pass. EL complained that he was *locked-up* in an old-folks home. I told him this was a temporary situation and soon we would see this as a testimony.

He began to complain about the CNA's, doctors, nurses and dietary. I had to be kind to the staff for both of us, giving thanks and praises for their care. Eventually EL followed suit.

*Affirming – the ability to encourage others and praise of who they are in God.
EL vowed that he did not want to be appointed by the Bishop to a pastoral position. He wants to just travel with me and be *free* the rest of his life. It is fine for a retired couple to travel, relax and savor the fruits of labor; but not because they feel useless. I told EL that his ability to minister was vital for such a time as this.

I affirmed the ability he has to help young men have structure in their lives. He has a pastor's heart, and that will help lives in more places than just behind a pulpit. I brought to EL's attention how many people look to him to be a listening post for matters of the heart. I encouraged him that God has things for his life that are new and fresh. I ministered to EL and my heart became energized.

*Nurturing – the ability to facilitate growth, acceptance, affirmation, grace, and love.

It has been said, men sometime look for wives that remind them of their Mama. I believe that saying has validity from the aspect of nurturing. To nurture and be a wife puts a me in a balancing act. I feel caught in a cycle of appreciation and abuse.

Fostering combines caring with confrontation. Mothers have been known to say; "this whipping is hurting me more than you". EL does not like to be confronted. He does like being cared for. To help him grow physically stronger, I wean him from waiting on him hand and foot.

As strength comes, and I pull back, then whining sets in. I must confront him with, "You can do it." "Try it." and as Dr. Wallace says, "No." is a compete sentence. Therefore, nurturing is a very close kin to being a good wife.

*Liberating – the ability to help others recognize the sources and causes of oppression.

I will say, liberation is like cutting the apron strings. EL has moved from bedridden, to sitting up, to using a walker, to strutting a cane. That is progress. On an emotional level EL is making strides from mind oppression.

I call him ⚡uperman, and he calls me "Wonder Woman." This kind of talk is nothing new for us. However, at this time, these words tend to give inner strength more than being flirtatious.

*Empowering – the ability to emphasize what is presently good and valuable in another.

Recently that I came to grips with how

empowering is enabled. There is a Scripture that helps me, to help others, simply by putting them first in compliments.

Philippians 2:3 says

Let each esteem others better than themselves.

I give EL accolades for mundane and important things he says and does. In response, I see and hear him stretching to be more self-confident. I am delighted and I feel more secure, with him being more secure. There is a reciprocal principle in the empowering process. His confidence increases my security level. We have weathered storms of life and had a myriad of reconciliations. Our enduring relationship has been established by the Word of God.

As a result of CPE my knowledge and actions have changed for the better. I am more confident to stand in the office of a caregiver. I know my listening skills have been enhanced and will be an asset in all communication exchanges. And, I am actively working on empowering people as oppose to giving my concluded answers to their situations.

Printed by permission of EL

*All CPE definitions are Wallace

Discuss How You Handled the Stresses of Someone and of Yourself While Being a Caregiver.

_____

_____

_____

_____

_____

_____

_____

_____

_____

_____

_____

The Marriage Bed

"Irreconcilable differences" become reasons for marriage breakups; no-fault divorce allows marriage to be terminated quickly and legally when one or both of the spouses simply lose the desire to stay together. Marriage the permanent union created by God, is treated more and more as a temporary arrangement of convenience"
Collins p. 545

Many times a power struggle takes place in discussions. Communication will turn argumentative. The need for reconciliation tells you one thing for sure ~ there was a problem. Not just an irritation, but possibly, a deeply rooted foundation. Individuals have parental, religious and community influences. These ideals must be brought to the surface and dealt with openly. When the couple is honest, with each other, they can collaborate on the conflict. With both sides involved in discussion, a successful decision will be made. The results will be good for both people. Marriage is a work in progress. There is not a fixed formula to a successful marriage.

High quality communication is a major key to keep marriage healthy. Taking time to put things in perspective helps temper the atmosphere and bring good results. Sometime stepping away from each other, for a short breather is necessary. Praying together is powerful in heading off problems and reconciling troubles. Embracing forgiveness is vital to conflict resolution and maintaining a peaceful home.

The Marriage-bed is not the place for rectifying marital struggles. Personal attentiveness builds a  strong bond in marriage. Leisure time, getting away from the hustle of everyday life helps couples to reach peace. Security and stability are critical elements in conjugal relationships.

Romanticism leads to good feelings and build lasting relationships. Sensual loving words ease stress and gentle touches relax muscles. Unmistakably, healthy lovemaking and peaceful sleep belong in the marriage bed. There, sex is undefiled. There, the mind, body and soul are strengthen. Solomon and spouse sweet talked to each other in excerpts from Solomon 1-8:

"Let him kiss me with the kisses of his mouth:
He shall lie all night betwixt my breasts.
His left hand is under my head,
and his right hand embrace me.
Sweet is thy voice,
Thou ravished my heart, my spouse.
Thy lips, O my spouse,
and honey and milk are under thy tongue:
This is my beloved, and this is my friend.

I know, right? Solomon really had a way with words. God anointed him to be the very first crooner. He and his spouse were together and they were not ashamed. Couples are allowed to explore and decide their own emotional, physical, and spiritual fulfillments in the marriage bed. If a spouse is uncomfortable or feels pain with love a making activity; that action does not belong in their relationship.

When both spouses are pleased with the love-making they engage in, no one else is relevant. The pleasures of husband and wife are confidential. However, foreign objects, drugs and sadistic acts are not part of Gods' of purpose in our lives or in the marriage bed.

Sex is coitus, physical union of male and female genitalia. It is accompanied by pulsing movements. That is basic intercourse and physical gratification. Godly love-making is much more. The two become one. Emotionally, the husband and wife share their expressions, warmth, love and trust. They know each other's heart desires and fulfill each other's needs.

The spiritual aspect of sex includes God. He is the one who created love-making and declared it 'good'. God made climax exciting and orgasmic waves enjoyable, with delightful tingling sensations. God's good pleasure is experienced throughout all parts of the body, and into the soul; because Holy Spirit is there!

In our marriage, it is very important for us to say, Thank you, I love you, and have long warm embraces, after love-making. A Christian married couple making love is a quality so indescribably delicious, that there is no real word. One flesh ~ one spirit, that ecstasy is

Super-cali-fragi-lis-tic-expi-ali-docious!

Discuss Ways You and Your Spouse Strive to
Preserve The Marriage Bed for Sleep and Sex.

_____

_____

_____

_____

_____

_____

_____

_____

_____

_____

_____

The In-laws

My Father and Mother-in-law is Gilbert and Dallas LeSure. 'Mah' and Pa stayed together in marriage over sixty-seven years; until death parted them. I was honored to tailor Mah's fiftieth wedding anniversary gown. Oh Happy Day!

Mah is truly, an original 'Old School' wife. She takes the prized care in attending to Pa's needs and desires. I saw her rise from bed to make fluffy, soft biscuits from scratch. She cooked cured bacon, fresh hen eggs and brewed coffee, all before the sun was fully up. With twelve children, she still grafted me in her heart, as a daughter. I love Mah.

Her demeanor is calm, warm, and accommodating. Mah never speaks loudly. To engage in conversation you must sit down, next to her. She softly touches and rubs my hand, with reassurance. I listen to her speak. She whispers good things in my ear. Her tender words are full of life giving treasure. Mah has a laugh that is hardy and nippy. She is quick witted and sober minded. I have learned by observation about being a loving wife. She is my wife role-model.

The role of mother is powerful when lived by loving example. Women who take time to teach their children will leave a legacy of strength and honor. What was good in the 1950's, is even better for the twenty-first century. Whether married, single, widow, or devoiced trustworthy mothers are priceless.

A few years ago, LeSure and I took Mah and Pa out on the town. We walked behind them and admired them walking together as one. They were side by side, looped at the forearms, each with a cane on their outer  legs. They marched in time to each other's swayed limp. Their beat that was in perfect sync.

~ ~ ~

"Not only does God call us;

He enables us to answer His call"

~ ~ ~

Elder Eddie Frank LeSure, Senior,

at the home-going of

~ ~ ~

Reverend Gilbert LeSure,

June 2013

How Has Your In-Laws or Extended Family Impacted Your Way Life in a Positive Way?

_____

_____

_____

_____

_____

_____

_____

_____

_____

_____

_____

_____

Closet Prayers

At thirty years old, I had been married twelve years. We had four children. I was a babe I Christ; born-again less than one year. Eager to know God's Word and practice it. My heart reacted to the Word like a sponge; it soaked it up. After reading, Matthew 6:6, I took that scripture to heart, literally.

when thou pray,
enter into thy closet;
and when thou hast shut thy door
pray to thy Father which is in secret;
and thy Father which see in secret
shall reward thee openly.
Matthew 6:6

New Christians are very precious. They walk in childlike, obedient faith. One day, I cleaned up my husband's small clothes closet. Then, I systematically arranged his pants, shirts and shoes.

 I could fit inside, kneel and close the door. That was my prayer closet. Many fabulous times were spent praising God, interceding and crying. I listened to for divine instruction, received needed help, and embraced spiritual peace. I depend on my Father to meet me in my secret closet. What a great growing time in my walk with the Lord.

Today, I have another prayer closet (though, He hears anywhere). The Lord still encounters me there and He rewards me openly. Jesus is my burden barer, my mind regulator and He breaks every yoke that tries to stronghold me into bondage.

The Lord yet works miracles and reconciles relationships. He saves to the uttermost and fills Believers with The Holy Ghost. Our mainstay is the infallible Word of God. As we pray, Holy Spirit reveals more understanding to us. We share

Truth to expose spiritual darkness and proclaim Jesus as Lord! The family cannot pray together, if they cannot stay together. I don't mean physically. Families need to stay together spiritually. No prayer-no power, much prayer-Much Power!

Father, I thank you for hearing and answering my prayers. Holy Ghost, I thank You, for an ear to listen and words to speak ~ in my secret closet.
In Jesus' Name.
Amen.

Speak About Your Designated Place
to Meet God in Prayer

_____

_____

_____

_____

_____

_____

_____

_____

_____

_____

_____

_____

Nurturing Nippers

Holy Spirit directed me in teaching our babies. I read the Bible to our children before breakfast. I explained Scriptures to them; as I learned for myself. One teaching method was singing passages, from the Bible, to familiar gospel melodies. Another technique was using verses as part of our daily living. For instance; I would wake them by quoting:

Isaiah 60:1

"Arise, shine;

the Light is come,

and the glory of the Lord,

is risen upon thee"

While eating, the kids watched children shows like Davey and Goliath. That animated program taught moral values on love, faith, and respect. They were trained with a Christian worldview.

We had joyful birthdays and family outings especially Easter and Christmas. At the end of a school week, I gave 'Happy Friday' gifts; wrapped or under their pillow. This is a love gesture, my daughter, Monika, now uses with her children.

We disciplined them to ask themselves, "How would Jesus respond?" When confronted with challenge, or tempted they had a foundation to reflect from. They were shown to share their possessions and time. Eddie and I demonstrated compassion to people in emotional pain. We consciously showed our children how to treat others. We lived the life we taught. We lived so our children could see the beauty of Christ in us.

Physical attractiveness does not compare to spiritual loveliness. Pleasing looks are skin deep; but acting ugly is to the bone. We taught them to look their best, but, not be prideful. We labor in expressing to them to keep their mind on Jesus because the mind is a continual battlefield.

As a man thinks, in his heart, so is he.
Proverbs 23:7

We model holiness in our home, church, lifestyle. We diligently pray with our children and love each one, unconditionally. As they grew Michael faithfully worked with youth, Frank happily sung in the choir; Monika was a Jr. Missionary, and Matthew is an anointed saxophonist.

We trained our children in the midst of other families who were living to have Godly families. Our ongoing prayer is that each child fulfills God's purpose for their life. Grandchildren are now here with their gifts. God instructs us with a promise;

Train-up a child, in the way he should go;
when he is old, he will not depart from it.
Proverbs 22:6

My best friend, Beverly, was my confidant while 'nurturing nippers'. Our lasting relationship is built on raising our children and developing our *'for better or worst'* marriages. We communed on everyday living issues. We learn many important life-lessons. Our insatiable love of crafting and entrepreneurship bonded us. Eventually, we entered a new stage of caring for elderly love ones. We yet strive to guide our grown children and grandchildren to trust, honor and love the Lord.

Four of our grandchildren spent the night with us recently. At bath time, the six year old was complaining and crying about mistreatment from the fifteen year old. When Bernadette was questioned about the problem, she tattled, "Monique won't let me have my way!"

Youth lash out not just to get their way but, some *because* they get their way. We need to rush back to basics of knowing the kids world, holding children to expectations, being aware of family dynamics and learning their interests and issues.

Youth have important questions of identity, who they are; how to relate to others; what they believe and where will they fit in? These questions must be answered openly and honestly, as part of their health, stability and  maturity. There is no better way to help our youth than by teaching them the principles of God.

Children dysfunction when they take on parental roles. Their hungry eyes search for instruction, discipline, purpose and hope. Many young people lack attainable dreams, positive self-identity, and strong support systems.

There are many who have had the advantages of being nurtured at home, wrapped by the community and trained in the way to go, but refuse to be obedient. Regardless of the family structure, living arrangements or conditions in the society some refuse physical and spiritual freedom.

There is no excuse to exist without Jesus. Excuses are non-compliance tools. They are flat out refusals to comply in obedience of God. Families of all types must be reconciled to each other to prosper. We need the forgiveness and redemption of God no matter what our station is in this life.

How Have You Nurtured
or Helped Train a Child?

_____

_____

_____

_____

_____

_____

_____

_____

_____

_____

_____

My Destiny with Destiny

At a levy base, on the muddy Mississippi River; I strolled in Moon Landing Park. I played on a rubber-seat swing set. I gripped the links of the  chains and swung back and forth, higher and higher. At the cardinal age of 59, it felt pretty good and reminded me of my youth. Then, I rested at an aluminum picnic table. I sat silently, shadowed by the strong massive cottonwoods. Trees so tall, they seem to brush bottoms of white cumulus clouds floating overhead.

I reflected on experiences and challenging work while at Destiny. I had a desired closer communion with the Father, more spiritual warfare tools, and formal Bible training. Today's ministry careers demand credentials, not just anointing. We are not all scholars but, we can all study the Word!

Drs. Penson and Blitch are to be commended, for reaching a lofty goal. They established The Destiny of H.O.P.E. Bible Institute, in Fox Valley. They successfully brought a new, needed and helpful accredited school to the region.

Expectancy of revelation from God, and foundational Bible knowledge charged the learning atmosphere. God's Glory was continuously present. Comradely among staff and peers was alive and healthy.

Dr. Williams skillfully taught my Masters' program. He dove headlong into fast-paced lessons and profound books, without pause or delay. Tests were intense. Early-on, Professor Williams warned; "Only the strong survive." He was right. We spent countless hours studying unfamiliar material, diligent research, writing and rewriting. Classmates collaborated online, texting, conference calls and around my kitchen table. A peer described our final exam as,

"Feeling like going to the electric chair!"

It worked out for us all. I was conferred Valedictorian of my Master of Divinity class 2012. Others were happy I had finally graduated too. Rosie wrote:

"I have known Mary LeSure for many years; we have shared confidences, life experiences, and traveled together. She is confident, interesting and transparent. Mary has demonstrated interpersonal skills, working with the public and speaking to diverse groups. She has coordinated business-related seminars and special events requiring intricate timing. Mary is dedicated to achieving her goals, continuing to work for nearly ten years, to earn her degree in Human Resources. I am so proud that she has now completed her Masters work, and graduated Valedictorian of her class."

Rose L. Tooley, DRE

Educator,

Philadelphia, Pennsylvania

Professor Jones, is a sober minded intellectual, perpetually prepared. He cordially connects with students, inducing an environment of scholarship. The program lessons, tests, and research papers were strenuous. Jones assured us by answering inquiries with knowledgeable, concise explanations.

Van Til's apologetics immersed colleague Berry and me, into ocean-deep studies. We literally danced around the table, at completion of the book! But, there was a 1,000 page *elephant*, in the room. Dr. Jones said, "Just eat it one bite at a time." Sure enough, the concentrated, Christian Counseling book was slowly, but surely, consumed. Alas, a 20,000 word dissertation waited in the wing.

Berry and I tolerated the ambiguity, asking ourselves; "What are we doing here?" By God's grace, prayers in Jesus' name, help of Holy Spirit, Visine, and Advil; we made it, as the first Destiny of H.O.P.E. Doctoral graduates! Yet, as Paul said, in: Philippians 3:8

I consider everything else, as dung,

pure worthless, and count it all loss,

to have the excellent, priceless privilege of

knowing Christ Jesus, as my Lord.

It is an advantage to have the highest attainment in education; a terminal degree. Yet, even this is as excrement when compared with the priceless privilege of knowing Jesus as Redeemer.

What Steps Have You Taken to Make Formal Bible Education Part of Your Life?

_____

_____

_____

_____

_____

_____

_____

_____

_____

_____

_____

Chapter Three

Butterfly

Gods' Purpose for His People
Witnessing to The Lost and
Edifying The Body of Christ

God's Purpose for His People

"Why am I on Earth?" This question finds meaning when we acknowledge God's purpose for each life. Learning His plan and walking in His way makes living worthwhile. We experience abundant life while living in His design.

A cocoon is not a resting place. Inside the cocoon is a lot of activity. The caterpillar is transforming into a new creature. This requires that the old caterpillar body is broken down and turned into something new. A caterpillars digests itself from the inside out. The same juices it used to digest food, as a larva, are now used to disassemble its own body. The fluid breaks down the old caterpillar body into undifferentiated cells, called imaginal cells. They can become any type of cell, for the new body. Imaginal cells form eyes, antennae, wings, legs mouth parts and genitalia. The larva emerges from its cocoon a new creature. The mature stage differs greatly in form, from the caterpillar. The transformation features a narrow body, and a pair of clubbed antennae. The sensory appendage on the insects head, receives external stimulus. They have four broad, colorful marked wings. The caterpillar changes to a butterfly. The fluttering sections are clear and easily seen. It flies mainly in the daytime.

I emerged a new creature. In Christ I was born-again; changed from sinner to Saint. Yet, I strive to be more like Christ and proclaim the Gospel to unbelievers and edify Believers; God's purpose for my life.

I'm Coming Out!

Sowing Seeds for Souls

He that received seed into good ground
is he that hears the Word, and understands it;
also bears fruit, and brings forth,
some an hundredfold, some sixty, some thirty.
Matthew 13:23

 Currently, I live in an area of the country that has good growing soil. And the weather is very fine for fruitful production. Farmers fertilize, plant seed and harvest cotton, soy beans, wheat and corn. They maintain and rotate the crops several times in one season.

A sprout grows up into the air and a stem transports it to sunshine. It multiplies with more leaves. Underground, the root-hairs are strengthen and spread. They feed on water and minerals. Seed-leaves develop and nourish the baby plant. These healthy plants grow and bear much fruit.

While walking country roads, I see the bounty of sowing, watering, maintaining and God giving the increase. At each harvest time, the beauty of mature crops is a sight to behold.

Tall stalks of green corn stand like soldiers with victory-staff tassels. Soybean plants form bunches fit to display as a table centerpiece. The golden-ripe wheat shimmers as it sway in the breeze, distributing a real  calming fragrance. And, cotton; the king, so fluffy and stark-white it reminds me of many winters in knee deep frosty snow.

Our purpose is to help cultivate Godly habits. When faith roots are strong there will be perseverance when opposition comes. We must be unswerving in our personal convictions. We must protectively care for seeds of faith to grow to fruitfulness.

- Be Christ-focused not self-centered
- Be Christ's guidance not a control freak
- Have Christ's security not fear and rejection
- Have Christ's love not anger and bitterness

If we allow currency, possessions, or the lack of either to rule our lives, we will fall deep into a pit of danger. God entrusts us to use money, talents, and time to further His Kingdom work, of winning souls.

Interpersonal tensions, marital strife, business ventures and church families have all suffered due to greedy and harmful effects of mismanaged money. A decision must be made in one's true heart ~ love money, power, and possessions; or God and His Way.

Man's spirit salivates, as direct contact is made with God, our Father, His redeemed people. The Creator is Who we are truly hungry for. No one else and nothing else will satisfy our souls. He speaks to us, to guide us. That is the power beyond the five senses. That is the sixth sense! The Voice of God is calling you.

Deep within man's being, beneath the temporal five senses of touch, sight, taste, smell and hearing is a ringing more prompting than that of Pavlov's dogs.

How Has God Called You to Sow His Word

by Being a Witness to People?

_____

_____

_____

_____

_____

_____

_____

_____

_____

_____

_____

We Need A Church Home

There is an absolute must for a local church home. Believers need to share in corporate praise to God. Who is Worthy of all Glory and Honor. Church gatherings are a place where Jesus commands His sheep to be fed.

Jesus said to Simon Peter, "
. . . do you love Me?"
"Yes, Lord," he said,
"You know that I love You."
Jesus said,
"Feed My lambs."

Again Jesus said,
"Simon, do you love Me?"
He answered,
"Yes, Lord, You know that I love You."
Jesus said,
"Take care of My sheep."

The third time He said,

"Simon, do you love Me?"

Peter said,

"Lord, You know all things;

You know that I love You."

Jesus said,

"Feed My sheep.

John 21:15-17

At church we learn healthy patterns of being led by Holy Spirit.   Godly fellowship with other Christians is where young Saints can grow spiritually, by the experience of mature Saints. Congregations need all ages of life to be well rounded.

At church we learn how to get sanctified! That simply means 'set apart' for God's use and Glory. According to me, Saint is the root word of Sanctified. Christians are not sinners anymore, we are Saints!. We do not do what we used to do when we were sinners. All things become new. Our deliverance from sin, shame and guilt began a new life. We had a new appetite. Hungry for the Word of God, my husband and I joined The Temple of God Church under the charismatic leadership of Bishop J. Taylor, Jr. People flocked from miles around and packed the church.

He imparted doctrinal truth with good understanding. Bishop Taylor taught directly from the King James Version of the Holy Bible. He preached by God's anointing power. I sat close to the pulpit as possible and took composition books full of notes. Pastor Taylor's sermons always addressed the necessity of the Holy Ghost.

He dogmatically insisted that we need to be filled with the Holy Ghost. I was convinced that I would receive power to live right with God's Power living inside me. I knew I was saved but I wanted more. More power over my fleshly desires. I wanted the Holy Ghost power he preached about.

He made it clear that our body is the temple of the Holy Ghost. His sweat-soaked Jerry-curled hair was wringing wet; snot dripped, and spit flew. He jumped up in the air; his 200 pound body landed flat on his feet. The impact made a squishing sound, in perspiration soaked shoes!

That's where we rooted in God's Word. Belief in Jesus' life, death, resurrection and repenting of sin is salvation. It is the first fruit of righteousness. Sanctification is being set apart from sin, by the Holy Ghost. Holiness is the fruit of obedience. Saints are born-again people. All saints are commissioned by Christ to the fruitful ministry of winning souls for the Kingdom of God.

Missionary Palmer offered Bible study across the street from our home. LeSure and I found ourselves running to feed from her knowledge every Tuesday evening. Indicative of her teaching; once for a Christmas present, she gave us a vessel shaped like a bread basket; it held Scriptures. It sits on our dining table as serves as an aid to blessing our meals.

When introduced to the Missionary Society I fit right in. President, Missionary Taylor taught us how to serve outside and in church. I was a *real* Missionary. I had a mission to go and serve the sick and shut-in. Helping neighbors iron, clean, and babysitting was part of my growing up. Service entailed errands, visits to ailing folks, praying and reading the Bible. My teenage job of working in a nursing home was used as solid experience.

We carefully cleaned vessels and prepared elements for communion. We broke crackers for Christ Body, poured grape juice for His Blood and handled the sacrament table linens with precision.

The Lords' Supper was offered every first Sunday. Missionaries dressed in all white clothing, stockings, shoes, and gloves. The whole congregation wore white as a symbol of God's holiness.

Our music department was a heavenly melodic celebration. Anointed organist Tony set the tone from vivacious devotion to lively benediction. His nimble fingers glide effortlessly across the keyboard; directed by Holy Spirit. Drummers Hugh and Rob gave a steadfast rhythmical beat perfect for hand clapping and foot stomping.

Our Adult Choir enjoyed area popularity. The Choir featured; Dorothy, Allen, Rosalyn, Edward,  Jackie, Bertilla, Dossie, and Mary. They led songs adding fervency to the flames in the joyful hearts of worshippers. We song, laughed and cried, freely giving God praise that belongs to Him.

One Beacon News journalist, in a human interest article, reported that our church expressed emotionalism. On the contrary, the fact of *knowing* salvation, sanctification, and the presence of God's Glory is a spiritual position to shout about!

Pastor Taylor's group, The Dynamic Mighty Wings, was a thrill. The Gospel group was a favorite in the region. Vocals; Edward DeRamus, Perry Mamon, and Rev. Jettie Taylor, Jr. Percussion, Hugh Farrell. They sang with harmony, rhythm and  The Holy Ghost! The very first time I danced in The Spirit *(away from home)*, was at one of their live concerts. Glory! Hallelujah!!

Fellowship in the Body of Christ was joyous and communally united. Assembly with other churches in community, regional and interstate congregations were regularly received and well attended. All age groups were involved in the uplifting services. Great joy was spread abroad.

Ain't no party

like the Holy Ghost Party

'cause the Holy Ghost Party

don't stop!

Bishop Taylor wrote:

"I am Bishop Jettie Taylor, Jr., I have known Evangelist LeSure since 1983 when she and her family came and united with us. Evangelist LeSure is a wonderful person, and her character is outstanding. She has a good report with people and everyone she come in contact with. I find Evangelist LeSure teaching abilities to be superb. She is our head Sunday school teacher, Bible teaching assistant and has a number of years of experience. Evangelist LeSure is an excellent Minister of the Gospel, eloquent speaker and good expounder of The Word. Her teaching abilities is 'Just God Gifted.

Christian Education has taken many forms in my life including; guest speaker for numerous conferences, various worship services, door and street witness, mentor, and labors of love. Foremost, is my desire for souls to be saved and people to be delivered. In Bishop Bonner's Jurisdiction, of the Church of God In Christ; it is a pleasure to prepare and deliver theme sensitive messages at district meetings. Bishop wrote:

"Evangelist Mary LeSure is licensed under the leadership of The Sixth Jurisdiction of Illinois as Evangelist Missionary. She has served faithfully with us and is doing the work that God has assigned to her hands to do. She has demonstrated through her behavior that she is a woman of distinction and has the God-Given ability to work with a large group of individuals. Evangelist LeSure has the education and will provide moral strength for production and will contribute to members of society."

Bishop William Haven Bonner,

I enjoy writing features in the Daily Devotional Guides, of the 'Secret Chamber', published by the African Methodist Episcopal Church. That was an exciting opportunity given to me, by a millinery client, Dr. Julia Wade, Memphis, Tn.

Pastor and Lady Grant, of New Jerusalem Church, positioned me as Sunday school teacher. Delivery style was developed while using national study guides, reference aids and illustrative supports. It introduces historical information and acknowledges archeological findings; that clarify passages. The class is energized to participate. Lessons help scripture relate to todays' life and closing prayers affirm God's principles.

Pastor and Evangelist Mamon, at New Faith Temple, appointed me Bible study teacher. I used various Bible versions. It was fun to demonstrate with props, they enriched presentations. This was a significant opportunity in my teaching ministry. The opportunity allowed my development, of theological curriculum, in a systematic manner. Courses included; projected lessons, study questions and quizzes.

The designation enhanced my research technic. Pastor Mamon ordained me, Evangelist. Recently, My best friends Mom, Evangelist Long was funeralized. When I returned home I looked at a picture of my ordination. Five of the eight people on that picture are passed from this life; Evangelist Donelson, Evangelist Long, Elder Yearly, Elder Walker, and Elder Hampton. The three that remain are Elder LeSure ~ my husband, Pastor Mamon and myself. No man or woman knows the day or the hour the Lord will call. Jesus said He must be about His Fathers business, so must I, so must we. This book is part of doing my Kingdom work, while I yet live. Pastor Mamon wrote:

"I've known Evangelist LeSure for approximately twenty-five years, and her character is impeccable. She is a very conscientious person and takes considerable pride in whatever she is assigned to do. Her Christian character can easily be recognized in any aspect of her life. She is a vital part of this ministry, and presently assigned to the position of Director of Christian Education, and Superintendent of Sunday school. Teaching is her forte."

"The Village Vision" is the theme at Covenant Church. I was Director of Christian Education under qualified leadership of Senior Pastor and Pastor Nabor. The goal is to raise a community of faith walkers. We envisioned spiritual growth, by providing theological and cultural education while working with all ages.

The Christian Education ministry is not a one person job. Qualified staff is needed in key places to do implement and oversee curriculum of the church and do effective work. High standards are an intricate part of the department. Each staff member must know their gifts and operate to the fullest in their anointing. The Pastors and Director are responsible to appointment of staff. Christian Education goals are to organize, plan, and implement knowledge through Bible study, discipleship training, and other educational outlets. Students grow in understanding the gospel and related daily living. Practical diligence enables holistic life ~ physical, social, emotional, financial, spiritual and intellectual.

Bishop and Mother Taylor assigned LeSure and me to establish compassionate, spiritual leadership relations with all children and teens of the Temple of God Church. We and developed classes, activities and excursions. We were awarded "Outstanding Youth Pastors". Pastor Taylor entitled us:

'A Husband and Wife Team for the Lord.'

We enthusiastically worked with the married couples. Ministry was comprised of marriage seminars and a special annual dinner, inspiring people to *live in love*. One February, LeSure and I attended a Valentine Day dinner with my brother, David and his wife, Sandra.

Their union is a fine example of holy matrimony. They work together in the natural, with tangible prosperity. The oneness of their Spirit yields commendable fruit. The outing was a romantic evening for couples. It was oodles of fun. We won a prize in a marital game!

We instituted the occasion in our local congregation. The enjoyable 'Sweetheart Dinner' was well received. It became popular in our area. The function strengthened local churches. The family is the foundation of any community and this event supports that structure. The 'Black Tie Affair' includes: The Marriage Game, Vow Recommitment, and Husband/Wife Speakers. Our happy experience conceived and gave birth to another ministry! That ministry is called:

"Walking Together"

We offer pre-marital counseling and marriage seminars. Single persons benefit from pre-marital Christian counseling that supports a healthy way to start a marriage. It encourages people to evaluate the spiritual fruit in mate selection. Married couples are encouraged to walk in love for better or for worse, for richer or poorer, in sickness and in health, to love and to cherish each other. Eddie and I spent fruitful years in evangelizing and planting churches. The Lord blessed us to cultivate fruits of healing, deliverance, marriage revival, and souls saved.

We were privileged to connect with Pastor and Lady Gage, in the United Methodist organization. Pastor Gage is a mentor to me. They shepherded several congregations in various towns. LeSure and I began teaching Sunday school, at churches not on their preaching route. A few churches changed from circuit schedules to weekly services!

Expound on How You Have Learned
and Served in Your Local Church(es).

_____

_____

_____

_____

_____

_____

_____

_____

_____

_____

_____

Do the Work of an Evangelist

It was a quiet, smoldering summer morning in rural Galena, Mississippi. I lay still, pondering; drifting with the settle motions of our waterbed. I meditated on a revelation the Holy Ghost gave my soul in the wee hours of the morning.

I had come on this mission as licensed Missionary, now, the Lord called *me* to be an Evangelist. My spirit race with excitement!

The feeling was more special than high school graduation, getting married, or having babies. It was like ~ accepting Jesus as my Savior and receiving The Holy Ghost, all in one experience! I floated while dressing. I pranced doing domestic cleaning, when a knock on the screen-door drew my attention.

Two Caucasian men stood in the sunlit doorway of our single-wide trailer. They wanted to talk about

Jehovah.　The feeling was absolutely mutual! Jehovah Jireh is my provider.　Jehovah Rapha is my Healer. Jehovah Shalom is my Peace.

We sit in my tiny living space.　I listened.　They told me about the 'New Kingdom on Earth.'　It sounded good, but, they did not mention how they would get to be a part of that kingdom.　I felt Holy Ghost Words rising up to my throat.　A break came in their speech.　I evangelized Jesus' life, death and resurrection.

They refuted what I was saying, but, could not stop my preaching!　They dashed to the door.　I was in hot pursuit, with my Bible in hand!　The pair sped across the grassy hill in the front yard, omitting the dirt-dug steps, my husband made.　I ran behind them, shouting,

"Wait!

Wait!

Jesus is God!"

Those men were Jehovah's Witnesses. Jehovah's Witnesses believe salvation emphasis is on works. Christians believe Gods' plan for salvation, by His Grace through faith, in the finished work of Christ on Calvary. We believe Jesus is The Only Way. Jesus, Himself said:

I am the Way, the Truth and the Life:
no man cometh unto the Father, but by Me.
John 14:6

Jehovah's Witnesses members are sincere in their practices, but, they are sincerely wrong. They deny the Holy Bible is God's Word of authority, Salvation by Grace through faith in Christ, the Trinity, eternal punishment of Hell's fire, and the Deity of Jesus.

There is an adage:
"The Word will draw `em or drive `em."
Well, that day it drove them!

What Ways Has Holy Spirit Equipped and Led You To Do the Work Of an Evangelist?

_____

_____

_____

_____

_____

_____

_____

_____

_____

_____

_____

_____

Teach All Nations

This past spring, we moved to Tunica. The only persons we knew, in the region, are our daughter, and her family. I had a lofty goal to open Destiny of H.O.P.E. satellite campus.

Classes offer accelerated Bachelor, Master and Doctorate programs. Scheduling is for active lives. Prices are affordable to attain accredited seminary degrees. Whether lay-person or minister, the curriculum is a system of understanding major doctrines of God's Word. Career positions require degrees job postings. Ironically, the average local church does not advocate formal Biblical training or seminary education.

We hit the ground running; visiting churches, schools, local events, and community centered groups. We met many people, made announcements and passed out loads of flyers for the Bible school. I sent numerous letters and made tons of phone calls. Dozens were interested as potential students. Several had good intentions and paid registration fees.

Minister Hayes, took the reins and led others to Destiny. Her friend, Evangelist Simmons came on-board willing and ready to study. Pastor and Lady Fullilove, were enthused students. They graciously extended Belmont Church fellowship hall for classes.

Truly, Holy Spirit has bonded us. Thank You Jesus, for favor. The arduous work and God's favor paid off. I was satellite founder and professor 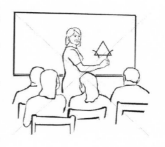 for the Destiny, Mississippi campus. God's merciful preservation and preparation has brought me to that place. My life's experience is in the purpose of teaching God's Word. I study and teach curriculum with integrity and live Christian values a daily basis.

Doctrinal training is necessary for healthy individuals, peaceful family home, social relations, organizations and political entities. God's guidelines are vital to enlighten souls and impact the evolving new world order. 'Apologetic' originates from Greek ~ *Apologia*: to defend. Early Christians defended their faith against critics who denounced the Gospel.

Through the ages, focus giving reasons for our hope is founded in Jesus as Lord, and soon coming King! Little did I know, that faithful day of witness to those two Jehovah's Witnesses, in 1988, I made a stance as an Apologist. They sprinted from my mobile home because of God's Truth. We ought to be zealous for Christ to fulfill the Great Commission given to all Believers worldwide.

Go ye into all the world,
and preach the Gospel
to every creature.
Mark 16:15

My Christian experiences rise and fall realistically. There are times, in my life, of great despair and almost debilitating utter weakness; those conditions have their place. They do not destroy my heart nor annihilate my soul. Holy Spirit in me, is greater than circumstance that affect me. He brings well-being back to my essence and gives me strength to rejoice!

Insights I have are intuitive capacities that I must learn to hold close to my chest until 'Kairos' – God's timing. Many times I have been premature on sharing a God-given discernment; to see disastrous results. I have to come to grips with the fact that just because I have gain an accurate and deep understanding of a thing or person; that does not give me the clearance to blurt it out. I am working on giving my thoughts careful consideration before saying what I am thinking.

How Has Holy Spirit Equipped and Led You To
Teach Starting at Home and Then Going Out.

_____

_____

_____

_____

_____

_____

_____

_____

_____

_____

_____

_____

The War Is On

With God's Word, we usher lost souls to Jesus Christ, through the power of Holy Spirit. The mission is to persuade unbelievers to Saving Grace and edify Believers. We want to help save many warm blooded people as possible.

Beelzebub's privates, corporals and sergeants have invaded men's souls with hostile intentions. But, the lieutenants, captains, and generals of El-Shaddai responds with a readiness that will prove to be a carnage ending to our adversary, for eschatology declares, 'their doom is set'.

God has preserved and prepared us for the purpose of winning souls for His kingdom. We need to be relevant on current issues of everyday life and world events. It is our responsibility to correlate those concerns to Bible Truths, including eschatology. That is, death, judgment and afterlife; particularly the Second Coming of Christ.

Get Ready!

Get Ready!

Get Ready!

And then, help someone else get ready.

Don't wait until the battle is over to shout, because

we know in the end, we are going to win, because

Jesus has already won.

Behold, I come quickly; and

My reward is with Me,

to give every man

according as his work.

Revelation 22:12

What Have You Done and How are You Helping

Others to be Ready for Christ's Second Coming?

_____

_____

_____

_____

_____

_____

_____

_____

_____

_____

_____

_____

Works Cited

Henry, Matthew and Thomas Scott. <u>Commentary on the Holy Bible</u>. Matthew through Revelation, Matthew 23:18-23, pages 66-67

The Holy Bible. <u>King James Version</u>. Nashville: Thomas Nelson Incorporated 1976.

Reedy, Elizabeth A. Ph.D. RN. "<u>Intensive Hospital based Care of Infants in Twentieth century America</u>". Penn Nursing Science University Pennsylvania School of Nursing.

Gamble, Kenny, Leon Huff, and Anthony Jackson. (The O'Jays). "The Love of Money." *Ship Ahoy*. Gamble and Huff for Philadelphia International Records, 1973. 'CD'

Collins, Gary R. <u>Christian Counseling a Comprehensive Guide</u>. Nashville: Thomas Nelson 2007.

<u>Taber's Cyclopedia Medical Dictionary</u>. Edition 14 Illustrated. F.A. Davis Company 1981

<u>Religion and American Cultures.</u> An Encyclopedia of Traditions, Diversity, and Popular Expressions. Volume One. Laderman, Gary, Leon Luis

<u>The Holy Bible</u>. Old and New Testaments in the King James Version.

Bfhu.wordpress.com/2007/04/21/why-do-catholics-pray-to-mary/ apologeticspress.org

<u>Clinical Pastoral Education</u> A Survival Kit. CPEO Equipping leaders to serve God's people. Copyright Brenda Perry Wallace 2017

Go Ye, and Teach All Nation

Matthew 28:19

Dr. LeSure Teaching experience spans over three decades, several states and numerous venues. Opportunities include study groups, conferences, revivals, congregations and schools.

She is a Born-again Christian, ordained Evangelist, licensed Reverend and anointed Bible Teacher. She earned her Doctorate of Divinity as conferred Valedictorian.

Professor LeSure is the founder of Destiny of H.O.P.E. Bible Institute, Mississippi satellite campus. She LeSure offers her God given gifts to minister as Convention Speaker, Christian Counselor, Bible Teacher, Evangelist or Author.

for Scheduling:
Phone 662-551-0556
bibleteacher1983@att.net

DESTINY OF H.O.P.E.

Christian Bible College, Mississippi Satellite Campus

Destiny provides courses that meet needs of all Christian Workers. We maintain high educational and spiritual standards. We progressively operate in a Biblical manner and academic excellence.

Destiny offers accredited Theological, Christian Education, and Ministerial studies. Students' attain knowledge to communicate clear and relevant understanding of the Bible.

Scheduling is designed for active lives. Accelerated classes are once per week for three hours. Prices are affordable to attain accredited seminary degree in one calendar school year.

Bachelor of Theology
Master of Divinity
Doctorate of Divinity

H.O.P.E. ~ *Helping Our People Excel*
Call Dr. LeSure for Your Registration
662-551-0556 ~ bibleteacher1983@att.net

"Two Walking Together"

Pre-marital Counseling and Marriage Seminars

Imagine learning powerful ways to head-off physical and emotional pits that cripple and destroy marriages.

Imagine working *together* with tangible prosperity and oneness of Spirit with healthy fruit.

Imagine understanding a spouse's character and properly dealing with their needs to heal fellowship.

Imagine knowing major keys to keeping your marriage strong and richly established.

Imagine your marriage reconciled after a devastating hurt, separation or divorce.

Single persons benefit from pre-marital counseling. Start your marriage with a Godly fruit selection.

The family is God's institution and the foundation of our community. Eddie and Mary have 46+ years of marriage to help you.

Rev. Eddie Frank, Sr. and Dr. Mary Elizabeth LeSure
'Husband & Wife Team for the Lord.'

Can Two Walk Together, Except They Be Agreed?
Amos 3:3

Please designate a date for your congregation
662-551-0556 or bibleteacher1983@att.net

Revealing Revelation

This seminar educates attendees with clear understanding of the mysterious Book of Revelation. The three-hour conference teaches you history's end and subsequent eternity.

- ❖ The Seminar flows in story-plot style.
- ❖ Old Testament precepts and prophecy is opened.
- ❖ Daniel and John descriptive symbols are revealed.

Testimonials include:
"Thanks, I see Revelation more clearly, now."
"I was comfortable asking questions."
"I enjoy teaching style, I am going to eat this more."
"I'm not afraid Revelation now."

Students completing the seminar receive a certificate. The lecture is non-denominational and open to anyone. An illustrated workbook is offered at the workshop.

Information and to schedule:
Phone 662-519-1724
bibleteacher1983@att.net

King of Kings and Lord of Lords
Revelation 19:16

Formal Education of

Rev. Dr. Mary Elizabeth LeSure

The Academy of Public Theology, Fairfield, AL
National Institute for Human Development
One Unit of Clinical Pastoral Education~2017

J D. Price Theological Bible College, Orlando, FL
Doctorate of Divinity Degree~2013
Christian Counseling ~ Conferred Valedictorian

Destiny of H.O.P.E. Evangelical Institute, Aurora, IL
Master of Divinity Degree~2012
Christian Education ~ Summa cum Laude

Northern Illinois University, DeKalb, IL
Bachelor of Science Degree~1996
Human and Family Resources
Individual Development

Wabaunsee Community College, Sugar Grove, IL
Associate of Science Degree~1993
Child Development

Made in the USA
Columbia, SC
27 September 2024

42538787R00114